Discovering

Michigan

Discovering
Michigan

Text: C. M. Gleaser
Concept and Design: Robert D. Shangle

First Printing October, 2000
American Products Publishing Company
Division of American Products Corporation

6750 SW 111th Avenue, Beaverton, Oregon 97008-5389

"Learn about America in a beautiful way."

Library of Congress Cataloging-in-Publication Data

Gleaser, C.M., 1961-
    Discovering Michigan / C.M. Gleaser.
        p. cm.
    ISBN 1-884958-60-5 – ISBN 1-884958-59-1 (pbk)
        1. Michigan—Pictorial works. 2. Michigan—Description and travel. 3.
Michigan—History. I. Title.

    F567.G58 2000
    917.74'0022'2—dc21   00-061826

Contents

Introduction

Michigan prides itself by having several symbols that represent the diversity of what lies within its borders. The State Flower is the Apple Blossom. The delicate white and pink bloom bursts forth in the spring, a common sight throughout the state. The apple tree, as an old staple fruit, is found on small farms, backyards and front yards of neighborly folks and is cultivated into a main cash crop in large commercial orchards in the state. The apple blossom can easily represent the entire fruit industry that is so abundant. Michigan leads the nation in sour cherry production and holds a strong position in apples, peaches and blueberries. Agriculture production, in general, places Michigan right up there with the best. Did you know that Michigan is a major growing state for asparagus? Other agricultural products are grown in rich soil producing abundant yields of grains and vegetables.

The warbling Robin represents the bird population in Michigan. But again, the Robin is a symbol of the diversity found here. Experience the wilderness areas where many birds make this place their home, and then listen for awhile. The solitude found in the pristine forests inhabited by the birds is often times the essence of what Michigan has to offer — a feeling of well being.

For the sportsman who enjoys going out for the hunt, there is a symbol that represents the diverse wildlife of Michigan, that is the White-tailed deer. There are many reasons to hunt for animals and it is not necessarily with a gun. The national forests within the state provide homes for many wildlife creatures: Black bear, coyote, otter, deer, beaver, mink, elk, moose and many more animals. And there are plenty of game birds such as grouse, ducks and geese. The hunter who carries a camera or binoculars has an opportunity to enjoy the animals in their natural habitat.

Most of Michigan's waterways allow fishing, and with the thousands of lakes, rivers, creeks and streams flowing through the state, the symbolic state fish, the Brook trout, can be easily located. Trout, Large-mouth and Small-mouth bass, the muskie and walleye, the Northern pike, and there is always the salmon, and the list goes on. What a wonderful place these waterways are.

The stately White Pine is the State Tree, a symbol of Michigan's earth bound beginnings. The foundation to Michigan's success was the tree. Most all of Michigan, the Upper and Lower peninsulas, have felt the strength of the lumber era. The conifer and deciduous hardwood trees gave Michigan a purpose, bringing a sound economic base to towns and the people who occupied the land. The felling of the trees brought the clearing of the land and the farmer moved in. As the lumber industry grew, people migrated to Michigan, their families grew and the need for supportive businesses developed. The lakeshore lands developed during the lumber era too, moving into a farming mode, then beckoned the tourist. Tourism provides a strong economic station in Michigan.

The strongest symbol of all is the State Flag. The blue shield is overlaid with a symbol of a rising sun over a lake and peninsula of land, "a man with raised hand and holding a gun represents peace and the ability to defend his rights. An elk and moose [support the shield and] are symbols of Michigan, while the eagle [above the shield] represents the United States." There are three mottoes inscribed upon the flag:

One Nation Made Up of Many Stars;
I will Defend;
If You Seek a Pleasant Peninsula, Look Around.

Michigan is a true homeland, where people live, and work, and play in a safe, secure setting. The diversity found within the confines of its boundaries describes the resilience of its people. If there is a challenge, it will be met and put to rest. Read on and discover what Michigan is all about.

What About Michigan

Michigan has more freshwater shoreline than any other state in the contiguous 48 states, some 3,200 miles. It consists of two peninsulas, the Upper Peninsula and Lower Peninsula. The Upper Peninsula is bound by Lake Superior on the north and the state of Wisconsin on the west; Lake Michigan and Lake Huron on the south; and on the east the Province of Ontario, Canada. The Straits of Mackinac separate the Lower Peninsula from the Upper Peninsula. The state of Wisconsin is on the west with Lake Michigan situated between the states, providing shoreline to Wisconsin and Michigan. Lakes Michigan and Huron provide a northern boundary, separated by the Straits of Mackinac. Beginning at a northern terminus and moving south, the eastern boundary is created first by Lake Huron; followed by the St. Clair River, Lake St. Clair and the Detroit River, all of which separate the Province of Ontario, Canada, from the United States, and finally by Lake Erie. The southern boundary is created by the states of Indiana on the southwest and Ohio on the southeast. All in all, Michigan consists of 56,809-square-miles of rolling plains, rising hills, productive farmland, forests, rivers, marshland and streams, lakes and those Great Lakes, taking in 38,192-square-miles of water surface. The extensive shoreline of Michigan requires lighthouse surveillance, necessary to protect the mariner navigation. There are 124-lighthouse locations, giving Michigan the honor of having more lighthouses than any other state.

Michigan can hold her own when it comes to having water within its borders. It boasts of 36,000 miles of rivers and streams. Lake Superior is the largest freshwater lake in the world, covering 31,820-square-miles. And Lake Michigan is the only one of the Great Lakes that is located entirely within the boundaries of the United States. It definitely can command respect regarding its size as its length is about 307 miles, its average width is 70 miles and its maximum depth is 923 feet. There are scores of waterfalls throughout the state, primarily in the Upper Peninsula. Statistics get confusing when in one documentation it states more than 150, then the next indicates 198, in the Upper Peninsula alone. There are folks discovering unnamed waterfalls on a regular basis.

Points of elevation in the state of Michigan are calculated based on mean tide at New York City. Lake Michigan's elevation is 581 feet, Lake Huron is 580 feet, Lake Superior is 602 feet and Lake Erie is 572 feet. Since the lakes are flat, knowing a starting point elevation makes it easier to relate to a height dimension of a mountain or terrain location.

The Upper Peninsula has rugged hills and mountainous terrain. Mt. Arvon, located in the upper northwest part of the peninsula is a few miles inland from Lake Superior and west of L'Anse, rises 1,979 feet. There are high rising bluffs, reaching 600 feet at the upper shoreline along Lake Superior, and the shoreline is more irregular and convoluted than the Lower Peninsula. In the western portion of the Upper Peninsula there are several places that reach a respectable height. For example, Negaunee has an elevation of 1,400 feet, Ishpeming is at 1,434 feet; farther west at Ironwood the elevation reaches 1,500 feet. In general the Huron Mountains in Marquette County and the Porcupine Mountains in Ontonagon County boast about having some of the highest elevations in the state.

The Lower Peninsula's elevation is quite varied. The shoreline areas are comparable to the height of the lakes. From Mackinaw City south the elevation increases to well over a thousand feet in many locations, tapering down to several hundred by mid-state. Gaylord's elevation is 1,348 feet, Grayling lists a height of 1,132 feet, and Mount Pleasant resides at an altitude of 761 feet. Flint records 800 feet, Lansing is at 843 feet, Ann Arbor is at 766 feet, Jackson is at 942 feet and Kalamazoo is at 792 feet. The land is rolling and verdant, rich in farms and small communities across the state and to the south, where it reaches the states of Indiana and Ohio.

Michigan's Upper Peninsula has been a world leader in the mining industry since the 1840s. In 1842 the Chippewa Indians ceded about 30,000 - square-miles of their Upper Peninsula land to the United States Government. The Native Americans were aware of the copper veins in the land. They had mined the copper for many years, using it to make tools. In fact, the ancient copper mines had been mined as far back as 1200 B.C. according to Michigan's Copper Mining History. When the land became a United States possession, professional miners and would-be miners rushed the area beginning in 1843. They traveled in by boat, landing wherever a ship could make a safe moorage on Lake Superior, such as Copper Harbor and Eagle Harbor. "All this copper was shipped out of the copper country on small (by modern standards) boats, down treacherous Lake Superior and finally through the St. Mary's River Canal at Sault St. Marie." Eighty-five percent of the nation's copper production came out of the Upper Peninsula in 1849. Michigan's Park Geology states, *"These were the richest deposits ever discovered."* "By 1900 the shafts of Keweenaw [Peninsula] were the deepest in the world." Copper Mining is not a major player anymore. Labor strikes, the Great Depression and the lack of purchase orders put the mines out of business. The employees moved away. The towns founded on the Keweenaw Peninsula by the mining companies are gone or considered to be ghost towns.

Iron ore was discovered in 1844 and mining began in 1846. Areas in the western Upper Peninsula were gorged with the ore, such as the Marquette

Range and Menominee Gogebic Range. By 1890 eighty-percent of the nation's iron ore was produced from Michigan mines in the Upper Peninsula. Competition entered the scene and wrestled the lead from Michigan, but the ore production has maintained a strong hold on economic input in the economy. "The mines increased production during both world wars. During World War II, mining companies explored new methods of processing large reserves of low grade ore. These deposits, mined from open pits and then processed to concentrate their ore content, constitute Michigan's ore production today."

Oil is a commodity not often associated with the state of Michigan. Of the 83 counties in Michigan, oil wells are located in 72 of them.

Now if the agriculture department of the state had its way, Michigan would be ranked "the best of the best" when it comes to producing commercial crops. And they have every right to state that belief. They make a fine argument: "Michigan is one of the nation's most diverse agricultural states. From navy beans near Saginaw to cherries in Traverse City, Michigan grows over 100 commercial crops, second only to California in variety." Now, isn't that something to boast about? In the meat, fish and dairy department, Michigan takes a seat right up front. Michigan's Traverse City shouts the honor of being the world's leader in sour cherry production, producing 75 percent of the nation's crop. As for blueberries, Michigan knows how to grow them, and really knows how to sell them. The Michigan Blueberry Growers Association "is recognized as the world's leading marketer of cultivated blueberries." There is wine production, forestry products, fruits and vegetables, honey and maple syrup.

There is a true *industry giant* that commands top billing on Michigan's stage of Economic Events. Do the following names mean anything to you? William "Billy" C. Durant and General Motors; Henry Ford and Ford Motor Company; Walter P. Chrysler and Chrysler Corporation (now known as Daimler-Chrysler); Alfred P. Sloan, Lee A. Iacocca. Buick, Reo, Maxwell-Brisco. Oldsmobile, Cadillac, Pontiac, Chrolet and Model T. And there are many more names that should be in this list, but it must be evident by now that these names are synonymous to the automobile. City names such as Flint, Dearborn, Detroit, Highland Park and Auburn Hills are deeply imbedded in the automobile industry. The terms *Michigan* and *Automotive Industry* have a certain *ring* to those people whose lives have been involved with them. The automotive industry has been and still is a far reaching one, way beyond the finished product that is driven down the road. Imagine the financial institutions, architects, building contractors and material supply companies, real estate companies, steel mills, component companies, clothing companies, insurance companies. The list of business entities touched by the automotive industry may be endless. And how many people are transported daily by a product of the automotive industry. It is obvious that the impact caused by this huge industry is great on Michigan.

Lower Peninsula

For a physical description, Michigan's Lower Peninsula is shaped like a left-handed mitten, with the thumb on the right, or for a direction sense, the eastside. The land touching the Great Lakes of Erie, Huron, and Michigan is primarily tourist oriented. Various manufacturing or agricultural industries have contributed greatly to the Lower Peninsula. History also has played a great part in what goes on in the state.

Taking a drive through communities is a good way to find out what is going on, and it is best to travel on roads that allow a "touring" mode rather than speed. The Interstate Highway will get you to your destination quickly, but sightseeing is not afforded the traveler. This sightseeing adventure will begin along U.S. Highway 12 at Dearborn, just outside the magic city of Detroit, located in the southeast section of the state.

Dearborn is the town Henry Ford made famous. The Model-T Ford did wonders for the community as well as for the people of the nation. The Henry Ford Museum and Greenfield Village provide an opportunity to learn about the development of the Henry Ford legacy and to learn about Dearborn. This is the largest indoor-outdoor museum in the nation. There is also the Henry Ford Estate along with the Automotive Hall of Fame.

Known as a city for industrial merit, Dearborn has maintained its identity despite the huge city of Detroit that pushes it boundaries.

Ypsilanti is just west on Highway 12 and is home to Eastern Michigan University. To the north is Ann Arbor, a pretty town and home to the University of Michigan. The University admitted its first students, seven in total, in 1841 with a faculty of two and was located on a 40-acre tract of land. Today the student population is referred to in the thousands (over 50,000), with three campus locations and some 5,600-faculty members.

An area known as the Irish Hills is about 40 miles west of Ypsilanti and is home to the Walter J. Hayes State Park, where recreational facilities are available plus camping areas. In the 1790s Father Gabriel Richards, who ministered to the local Potawatomi Indians, established a missionary community overlooking Iron Lake. In the mid-1840s Irish settlers added structures to the complex. Today the religious-devotional center provides an insight to early religious pursuit and is a place for reverie. Just west is Cambridge Junction where the Michigan Speedway is located. Exciting car races are held here, where deft driving skills are a must.

Traveling north on a short trip up U.S. Highway 127 is the city of Jackson. A political historic fact: in 1854 the party name, *Republican*, was adopted for the Grand Old Party during a state convention in Jackson. Besides that distinction, Jackson has a beautiful 530-acre park along with an historical museum, both named for Ella Sharp. She was a spirited community activist who willed her wood framed house and 530 acres of property to the city of Jackson in 1912, at the time of her death. Her expressed wish was that the gift be developed as a museum and park. The park includes all the amenities for family fun: hiking and biking trails, swimming and golf facilities, and for winter activities, it includes cross-country skiing trails. The museum delivers a 19th-century life style, with all the things a period village has to offer: a house, country store and farm equipment. From the 19th-century move forward to the 21st-century and visit the Michigan Space and Science Center in Jackson.

Upper Falls, Tahquamenon FallsState Park

Located in Tahquamenon Falls State Park, the Upper Falls on the Tahquamenon River drops nearly 50 feet and exceeds a 200-foot span across the amber waters of the river, "caused by tannin leached from the Cedar, Spruce and Hemlock trees in the swamps drained by the river." The Park is located within the confines of Lake Superior State Forest and Hiawatha National Forest on the Upper Peninsula, north of Newberry.

Photography by Shangle Photographics

Linden Mills, Linden, Genesee County

The town of Linden, named for the once abundant Linden tree that grew in the area, claims ownership to the historic Linden Mills, located beside Tupper Creek. Genesee County was first organized in 1836 and was given a name that means "beautiful valley." The large city of Flint, located near the center of the county, is the county seat of Genesee County. Linden is to the south of Flint.

Photography by Shangle Photographics

Father Marquette National Memorial, St. Ignace

Honoring the French Jesuit missionary and explorer who developed the first settlement in Michigan, Father Jacques Marquette has a history beginning in 1666. He lived among the Native Americans, learning many of the native languages before his death in 1675. Located within the confines of the Straits State Park, on a rise overlooking the Straits of Mackinac, is the New France Discovery Center and Father Marquette National Memorial. As stated by the National Memorial, the center "tells the story of that 17th-century missionary-explorer and the meeting of French and Native-American cultures deep in the North American wilderness."

Photography by Shangle Photographics

Marquette Harbor Lighthouse, Marquette, Upper Peninsula

The one and only red lighthouse in Michigan resides in Marquette on a stone bluff that projects out into Lake Superior, creating a small peninsula. This stately old building was constructed in 1866, replacing an 1853 wooden building. A second story was added in 1906. The light tower reaches an overall height of 89 feet above the waterline, with the actual structure height measuring 45 feet. Marquette has an interesting Maritime Museum that provides extensive history of the maritime community.

Photography by Shangle Photographics

Renaissance Center, city of Detroit

Located within the city of Detroit, these grand buildings are known as the Renaissance Center, where the "why and what for" are accomplished by such business giants as General Motors, who maintain their world headquarters here. Located on the southeast border of Michigan, Detroit meets Lake St. Clair on the east; Windsor, Ontario, Canada, is directly across the Detroit River in a southeast direction; and Lake Erie is to the south. Think of Detroit and the automobile industry comes to mind. General Motors, Ford Motor Company, Daimler-Chrysler, and Volkswagen of America all headquarter in Greater Detroit. This city has brought to the forefront a renewal in man's accomplishments, a true renaissance of ideas placing it as a major city in the world.

Photography by Shangle Photographics

Sand Creek at Lake Superior near Marquette

Quiet flowing Sand Creek empties into Lake Superior near Marquette on the Upper Peninsula. Many rivers, creeks and streams feed Lake Superior, making it the largest freshwater lake in the world. The city of Marquette, on the southern shore of Lake Superior, once a leading shipping center, was named for Jesuit priest Jacques Marquette who came to the Michigan Territory in 1866. The Marquette Maritime Museum, housed in a vintage 1890s building, features maritime heritage of Marquette and Lake Superior.

Photography by Shangle Photographics

Forty Mile Point Lighthouse, Presque Isle County Park, Lake Huron

This active lighthouse is located six miles northwest of Rogers City in Presque Isle County Park in northeast Michigan, along the western shore of Lake Huron. P. H. Hoeft State Park is nearby. The county has 72-miles of lake shoreline, providing four interesting lighthouses: Presque Isle Peninsula, Old Presque Isle, New Presque Isle, and Forty Mile Point. Rogers City, the county seat for Presque Isle, is a four-season vacation mecca for the sportsman; it beckons the relaxed lounging enthusiast in spring and summer; calls to the autumn-color sightseer; and provides for the wintertime athlete. Rogers City leads the world in limestone production, as it is home to the world's largest limestone quarry. *Photography by Shangle Photographics*

Grand Hotel on Mackinac Island

The remarkable Grand Hotel, debuting in 1887, is a *grand centerpiece* on historic Mackinac Island, located in Lake Huron immediately east of St. Ignace on the Upper Peninsula. The "famous front porch is the world's longest" at 660 feet, affording a *grand view* out onto the island and lake beyond. Mackinac Island is rich in historic flavor and an intriguing adventure for island guests. The pace of life is definitely slower here, as no automobile is allowed, other than emergency vehicles. Horse-drawn carriages are available for touring the three-mile long by two-mile-wide island. Bicycle tours and the old-fashioned walking tour is a quiet approach to experience some of the special locations on the island. Ferryboat transportation is available from Mackinaw City on the Lower Peninsula and from St. Ignace on the Upper Peninsula.

Photography provided by Grand Hotel, Mackinac Island, Michigan

Little Sable Point Lighthouse on Lake Michigan, in Silver Lake State Park

Typical of the lighthouse towers built in the 1870s, Little Sable Point Lighthouse stands at 115 feet, Lake Michigan's tallest operating lighthouse, spreading its beacon over the area since 1874. First fueled with oil, then kerosene, the light was electrified in 1954. Visiting the lighthouse allows a visitor to explore the spreading sand dunes along the shore, either by foot or by vehicle. Comfortable Silver Lake State Park provides an opportunity for hours of beach fun, either on Lake Michigan or along Silver Lake.

Photography by Shangle Photographics

The city of Detroit

Located along an exciting waterfront that creates an economic advantage most cities do not share, the city of Detroit takes advantage of the 27-mile-long Detroit River. The Port of Detroit states that "the volume of goods traded (by value) through the Port of Detroit places it second in the United States …." The Port of Detroit is a multiple recipient of the Saint Lawrence Seaway Pacesetter Award. As many as "1,441 foreign waterborne shipments [are] imported across its docks." Detroit is Michigan's largest city and boasts of being one of the ten largest in the United States. However, all of the communities around Detroit are an integral part of Detroit's success. The surrounding cities of Dearborn, Auburn Hills, Southfield, Troy, Harper Woods and Royal Oak are considered by many as *the cities* that create Detroit. Belle Isle, Detroit River's 1,000-acre scenic park, affords this excellent view of the city and also provides a respite from the hustle and bustle of a fast-paced life. The Detroit Zoological Institute oversees the Belle Isle Aquarium, one of the oldest continuously operating public aquariums in North America, and the animal zoo is a "13-acre facility that features an elevated walkway from which visitors can view exotic mammals and birds." Detroit recognizes its founding day as July 24, 1701, first settled by French fur trappers. Today the settlers of this industrial giant represent all ethnic groups from around the world.

Photography by James Blank

Fayette Historic Town Site, Garden Peninsula, Lake Michigan

Once the Upper Peninsula's most productive iron-ore smelting operation, with "two blast furnaces, a large dock and several charcoal kilns," Fayette was once home to nearly 500 people. The furnaces at Fayette operated for 24 years, producing "a total of 229,288 tons of iron, using local hardwood forests for fuel and quarrying limestone from the bluffs to purify the iron ore." The Jackson Iron Company, who owned the operation and named the site for their agent Fayette Brown, closed Fayette in 1891, "when the charcoal iron market began to decline." The area is now within the perimeter of Fayette State Park, providing excellent camping facilities, expanded picnic areas, and swimming and scuba diving in Snail Shell Harbor. Seven miles of maintained trails are available for summer hiking and are groomed in the winter for cross-country skiing. Boating in Big Bay de Noc is suitable for small boats and larger, deep-draft pleasure craft.

Photography by Shangle Photographics

Scenic farmland in Huron County

As the four seasons come and go, nature's pallet of color is broadcast over the land, providing a landscape unequalled. Here in Huron County, located in the tip of the Thumb on the Lower Peninsula in northeast Michigan, autumn hues are well displayed in great variety. Fertile farmland is abundant, producing grains, sugar beets, and beans, which includes "most of the world's supply of navy beans." Bad Axe is the county seat for Huron County, where many small communities thrive, each offering tidbits of musing information. Bay Port ships "tons" of fish to New York and Chicago, and Elkton celebrates its annual Autumnfest on Labor Day weekend (Elkton was named by W. J. McGillivray for his hunting success after he killed a huge elk that was tangled in his wife's clothesline). The town of Pigeon, as well as the river, received its name from the many pigeons roosting there and the town is touted as a place offering the "good life." The National Historic Register placed the sawmill chimney, built by the Stafford and Haywood Lumber Company in 1858 at Port Hope, on its List of important entities. The town of Ubly (originally spelled Ubley but misspelled on the depot sign, so it stayed that way) holds hot-rod races in the summer each Sunday. Huron County is definitely a good place to call home.

Photography by Shangle Photographics

Mackinac Island and boat harbor, Lake Huron

Island guests enjoy the manicured-green that sweeps the island's grounds down to the marina. Transportation to the island is by boat or airplane, either commercial or personal craft. A leisure cruise over the waters of the lakes, Huron and Michigan, can provide an exhilarating experience. The intriguing village on the island displays many authentic Victorian homes and shops, tirelessly maintained to protect the vintage history so important to the island's existence. Natural beauty is also a great part of Mackinac Island, providing pristine settings where solitude is available. The fabulous sunsets have the ability to renew "things lost" in our fast-paced life. Memories of horse-drawn carriage rides, leisure walks, and fun-crazed bicycle tours can bring you back to the island time and time again. At any time Mackinac Island provides an opportunity to enjoy the good life.

Photography by Shangle Photographics

Porcupine Mountains Wilderness State Park, Upper Peninsula

As described by Exploring the North Internet Services: "In this era, a true wilderness needs to be big in order to escape the inroads of civilization. This one is big with nearly 59,000 acres of brawling mountain rivers, lakes and dark stands of virgin hemlock, pines and hardwoods, the largest virgin hardwood-hemlock forest in the United States. Some of these forests' monarchs are 200 years old. The Porcupine Mountains consist of a series of undulating, irregular ranges whose slopes are covered with stands of virgin forest of the hardwood-hemlock type, with maple, birch, and basswood on the upper slopes through hemlock mixtures on the lower areas. Nestled within these ridges are the beautiful Lake of the Clouds and Mirror Lake. From these lakes flow the Big and Little Carp rivers down deep-cut gorges. These rivers rush through a series of rapids and falls to Lake Superior." *Photography by Shangle Photographics*

Old Mackinac Point Lighthouse, Mackinaw City

Located on the northern tip of the Lower Peninsula on the Straits of Mackinac, the Old Mackinac Point Lighthouse lost its prestigious position of power when the Mackinac Bridge was opened in 1957. Built to replace a fog signal that was constructed in 1890, this 1892 structure reveals marvelous character and carries a history of activities that have taken place since its construction. The lighthouse stands within a public park and adjacent to historic Colonial Michilimackinac, on the site of Fort Michilimackinac.

Photography by Shangle Photographics

31

Mackinac Island and boat harbor, Lake Huron

History pervades the very depths of Mackinac Island (pronounced Mack-in-naw), first settled by Native Americans and then the French and British who trapped for furs, taking wealth from the island. In 1780 the British built Fort Mackinac on Mackinac Island. Battles were fought here during two formidable wars for independence, the Revolutionary War and the War of 1812. Following the Revolutionary War, the United States owned the island, but during the War of 1812, the British recaptured ownership. However, in 1815 the British returned the island to the United States regaining Michigan's "Crown Jewel", Mackinac Island. The fort was abandoned in 1894 and relinquished to the state of Michigan. Three-miles long, two-miles wide and nine-miles around, this island of smooth gentle slopes, quizzical rock formations, ravines and caves invites would-be explorers to venture out and discover its secrets. *Photography by Shangle Photographics*

Manistee North Pierhead Lighthouse, Lake Michigan

Guarding the entrance to Manistee Harbor and Duncan L. Clinch Marina, this 39-foot lighthouse stands in the waters of Lake Michigan. The city of Manistee houses an inland marina and wide boat canal, edging city center. First occupied in 1790 by French and British fur trappers, Manistee took roots as a lumber center beginning in 1841 when a sawmill was built. A large salt mine was discovered in 1881 that is still producing the valuable mineral. Historic Manistee provides excellent insight to the area's history.

Photography by Robert D. Shangle

Miners Castle in Pictured Rocks National Lakeshore, Lake Superior

Any time is a good time to visit one of Michigan's more scenic locations. The nation's first National Lakeshore was established in 1966, preserving some 73,000 acres of Michigan's pristine beauty in the Upper Peninsula between Munising and Grand Marais along the shoreline of Lake Superior. Springtime provides a profusion of wildflowers; summer accommodates easy access to the nature trails through the forest to lakes and waterfalls. Autumn arrives with the crisp air so abundant in this northern latitude, creating a kaleidoscope of color; winter sets a cloak of snow on the landscape that creates a sculptured wonderland. The Visitor Centers provide extended information regarding self-guided tours, suggesting visits to Munising Falls, Miners Castle, and Sable Falls. *Photography by Shangle Photographics*

Bronner's Christmas Wonderland, Frankenmuth

It is *always* Christmas at Bronner's, the world's largest Christmas store, where browsing for the "just right" gift may take awhile, since there are over 50,000 items from which to select. In 1976 Michigan's governor designated Bronner's as an "Embassy for Michigan Tourism." First established by Lutheran missionaries in 1847, Frankenmuth has grown to be a Bavarian Community that displays its ethnic heritage in many ways. Architecture, special-events celebrations and the downtown area refer to "the old country." Frankenmuth is located in Saginaw County in east central Michigan, a few miles east of Saginaw. Before the German immigrants arrived, three groups of Native American people occupied the land: first the Sauk, followed by the Iroquois and finally the Chippewa. Fur trapping was once so profitable that John Jacob Astor's American Fur Company established here. The United States acquired the land through the signing of the 1819 Treaty of Saginaw.

Photography by Robert D. Shangle

Fort Michilimackinac in Colonial Michilimackinac, Mackinaw City

Much history has been experienced here in Fort Michilimackinac, beginning with the French in 1715. The fort was originally constructed by the French for use as a trading post and for the expansion of the fur trade; military purpose was a secondary plan. "Overlooking the Straits of Mackinac connecting Lake Huron and Lake Michigan, the fort served as a supply post for French traders operating in the western Great Lakes region and as a primary stopping-off point between Montreal and the western country." Following the French and Indian War the British won possession. Battles continued between the British and the Ottawa and Chippewa people. The British maintained control of the fort until its closure in 1781.

Photography by Shangle Photographics

USS *Silversides*, Muskegon Lake at Muskegon

National Historic Landmarks states that "No other WWII submarine remains that sank more [war] ships than the USS *Silversides*." On October 18, 1972, the USS *Silversides* was placed on the National Register and on January 14, 1986, listed as a National Historic Landmark. Built in 1941, the ship "was launched at Mare Island Naval Yard, California, August 26."

Photography by Robert D. Shangle

The Kellogg House, Battle Creek

The one-time home of William Keith Kellogg who, along with his brother, Dr. John Harvey Kellogg, discovered and perfected flake cereal, creating a revolution in healthy eating. The house is now the headquarters to the W. K. Kellogg Foundation, a philanthropic organization designed specifically to assist young people. The Foundation's literature states, "Even as a millionaire, he resided for years in a two-story stucco house on 256 West Van Buren Street in Battle Creek."

Photography by Robert D. Shangle

Historic Fort Wilkins, Fort Wilkins State Park at Copper Harbor

Created for the express purpose of protecting life and property during the beginning years of Michigan's Copper Mining boom, Fort Wilkins was a short-lived garrisoned complex. Built in 1844 it was abandoned in 1846 and re-occupied by military forces for a short period in the 1860s. The heritage of the fort has survived through the 19 buildings that display the frontier history. Twelve of the structures date back to the 1840s. Tours by period-costumed guides provide a hands-on interpretive excursion of the fort. There are exhibits and audiovisual programs exploring the routine life of a garrisoned soldier stationed in the rugged frontier. Fort Wilkins State Park, located along the rugged shoreline of Lake Superior at Copper Harbor, is on the Keweenaw Peninsula of the Upper Peninsula of Michigan.   *Photography by Shangle Photographics*

Sleeping Bear Dunes National Lakeshore along Lake Michigan

Sleeping Bear Dunes National Lakeshore extends 35-miles on the eastern shore of Lake Michigan and includes 71,187 acres. Ojibway Indian legend states that a giant mother bear lies sleeping on a high-rising knoll, waiting for her two cubs. She led them away from danger, swimming across the Lake, and when she reached the shore she rested. The cubs never reached her. They are resting as the two islands west of the mainland known as North and South Manitou, also part of the National Lakeshore. Climbing the giant sand dune within the park is a "must-do activity" for the hearty and a grand view for the sightseer. The Pierce Stocking Scenic Drive provides seven miles of nature's best. Hiking and cross-country ski trails cover 55-miles in the mainland park plus extensive hiking opportunities on the two islands. Fishing in the several inland lakes and in Lake Michigan is perfect, where water sports can take place. Hunting is possible in portions of the Park for deer, grouse, rabbit, and waterfowl. Three rivers in the park, the Betsie, Crystal and Platte, allow canoeing, kayaking and tubing. There are camping facilities located within the park's boundaries. The Philip A. Hart Visitor Center for the National Lakeshore is located in the village of Empire, about 25-miles west of Traverse City on the Lower Peninsula. *Photography by Shangle Photographics*

Seul Choix Point Lighthouse, east of Manistique on the Upper Peninsula

The words *Seul Choix* mean "only choice." There is a story told about French fur trappers who, several hundred years ago, were seeking shelter from stormy Lake Michigan waters. They found shelter at a point of land they named *Seul Choix*. A very fine lighthouse was completed in 1895 and stands today in full operation. The Seul Choix Point Lighthouse Park and Museum provide excellent historical facts.

Photography by Shangle Photographics

University of Michigan, Ann Arbor

The University of Michigan admitted its first students, seven in total, in 1841 with a faculty of two, and was located on a 40-acre tract of land. Today the student population is referred to in the thousands (over 50,000) with three campus locations and some 5,600-faculty members. The flag waves strong on the manicured campus with Burton Memorial Tower in the background.

Photography by Robert D. Shangle

Dutch Village at Windmill Island, Holland

Authenticity is most important at the Dutch Village, located in southwest Michigan, not far from the eastern shoreline of Lake Michigan. Dutch-costumed shop owners add to the authentic charm of the village that includes a wooden shoe-maker, food shops and an interesting museum, plus more, including a Dutch Theme Park. Anytime is a *great* time to visit Holland, but especially in mid-May when thousands of tulips are in bloom and the annual Tulip Time celebration is in full swing.

Photography by Robert D. Shangle

The *Madeline*, a 92-foot replica of an 1845 Schooner, Traverse City

Memories of the original *Madeline* have been saved through the reconstruction of the "mid-19th-century fore-and-aft schooner built by the Maritime Heritage Alliance" in Traverse City. History records indicate the original *Madeline* was built in 1845 in Fairport, Ohio, and "carried barrels of fish from Mackinac Island and other commodities to and from ports on upper Lake Michigan." Today the *Madeline* is used as an interpretive learning center, providing information regarding Great Lake maritime history.

Photography by Robert D. Shangle

Sardet Coast Guard Station, Muskegon

Muskegon on Lake Michigan is home to Sardet Coast Guard Station, always ready to provide the necessary protection to mariners. Listed as a Search and Rescue Detachment, the Mission Statement posted by the U.S. Coast Guard states: *"Our Vision: As a leader in the maritime community, we will creatively exceed the public's expectations ensuring expanding waterway operations are safe, reliable, and environmentally sound."* Photography by Robert D. Shangle

Downtown Square in Frankenmuth

In the heart of downtown Frankenmuth the Bavarian Inn, registered as a Michigan Historic Site, displays a true "Old County" architecture so expressive of European Bavaria. First settled by Germans from Bavaria in 1845, a religious zeal and the zest for life planted deep roots in this east-central town in Michigan. The fertile land of the area provided productive farming, so lacking in the homeland. Today, year 'round festivities are scheduled in Frankenmuth, providing good food, holiday excitement and excellent family fun.

Photography by Robert D. Shangle

Bond Falls, Upper Peninsula in Ontonagon County

North of Watersmeet on the Upper Peninsula, east of Paulding on U.S. Highway 45, is Bond Falls, located on the Middle Branch of the Ontonagon River in Ottawa National Forest. There is a maintained walking trail that leads to this expansive waterfall, which cascades down some 50 feet. "Portions of the Ottawa National Forest receive over 200" of snow annually." Melting water maintains a good year 'round flow for this beautiful waterfall, said to be one of the more photographed places in Michigan.

Photography by Shangle Photographics

Greenfield Village, Dearborn

This vintage steam-powered locomotive is among the many intriguing attractions and exhibits at Henry Ford Museum and Greenfield Village, the world's largest indoor/outdoor museum. Other sites in the Village include Thomas Edison's Menlo Park Laboratory, The Wright Brothers' Home and Cycle Shop, and the Noah Webster House, all part of an 81-acre complex established by automotive pioneer Henry Ford. The Henry Ford Museum and Greenfield Village were designated a National Historic Landmark, December 21, 1981; listed on the National Register, October 21, 1969; and placed on the State Register, September 12, 1963. The museum was dedicated October 21, 1929 and The Edison Institute opened in 1933.

Photography © Henry Ford Museum & Greenfield Village

Munising Falls in Pictured Rocks National Lakeshore, Upper Peninsula

Munising Creek drops some 70 feet over a sandstone cliff creating the picturesque Munising Falls. Located within Pictured Rocks National Lakeshore, the layered colors of the sandstone, ochre, tan, brown and green hues, add to the eerie shapes created by rock formations within the park.

Photography by Shangle Photographics

Michigan State University, East Lansing

Michigan State University was founded in 1855 as a land-grant institution. The campus encompasses 2,100 acres. Many of the university buildings are named for people who have been involved with the growth and development of the academic achievements of the school. As seen here, the building identified with Robert S. Linton Hall, "is named for education professor Robert S. Linton who as university registrar streamlined the registration process, introducing the IBM class enrollment card." *Photography provided by Michigan State University*

Farmland near Empire, northwest Michigan

Following the felling of the trees that blanketed much of Michigan, the land was cleared and many of the residents turned to farming. The rich fertile lands of Michigan produce abundant crops. If the agriculture department of the state had its way, Michigan would be ranked "the best of the best" when it comes to producing commercial crops. "Michigan is one of the nation's most diverse agricultural states."

Photography by Shangle Photographics

Portage Lake Upper Entry Lighthouse, F. J. McLain State Park, Lake Superior

Located in Houghton County on the Upper Peninsula, this historic lighthouse was originally built in 1874, following the completion of the Portage Lake Ship Canal in 1861. The Ship Canal opened a waterway between Keweenaw Bay and Lake Superior. The lighthouse was reconstructed in 1950. The F. J. McLain State Park is about eight miles north of the city of Hancock. In total there are two miles of sandy beach along Lake Superior within the confines of the State Park. Lake Superior is the largest lake in the world. Besides laying claim to two miles of shoreline that allows great summer fun, there are modern campground facilities, playgrounds, and hiking trails. Fishing, windsurfing and beachcombing fill hours of time for the visitor. Open year around, winter activities include cross-country skiing and snow-shoe hiking. The one activity enjoyed by all ages, any time of the year, is viewing the spectacular sunset. *Photography by Shangle Photographics*

Kellogg's Cereal City, USA ™, Battle Creek

"Celebrating the cereal industry story in a fun, educational and entertaining manner, Kellogg's Cereal City USA is a themed family attraction/museum. The interesting, interactive theaters, exhibits and games illustrate the affect the cereal industry, which began in Battle Creek during the early 1900s, continues to have on everyone's life daily. Opened in June, 1998, the International Association of Amusement Parks & Attractions (IAAPA) in late 1998 named it "Best New Product" for its innovative design...."

Photography provided by Kellogg's Cereal City USA

55

State Capitol, Lansing

Originally opened in 1879, Michigan's Capitol carries the honor of being listed as a National Historical Landmark. Restoration work was completed in 1992. "The interior of the Capitol is one of the best surviving examples of Victorian decorative art in the United States." On January 16, 1837, Michigan became the 26th state to join the Union. The appropriate state motto states: "*If you seek a pleasant peninsula, look about you.*"

Photography by Shangle Photographics

Old Mission Point Lighthouse, Grand Traverse Bay, Lower Peninsula

Located on Old Mission Peninsula in Grand Traverse Bay, the Old Mission Point Lighthouse has stood sentinel since 1870. This wood constructed lighthouse with a natural/emplaced foundation has a thirty-foot tower and was active until 1933. It was listed on the National Register in 1992 in the Historic Engineering & Industrial Sites listing. The National Maritime Initiative Lighthouse Sites states, "The United States has a diverse collection of lighthouse construction types. The majority of today's surviving 595 lighthouses are land based; close to a fourth have foundations built in the water. Lighthouses were built on land, in the water, on islands, on top of ledges and cliffs, on breakwaters and piers, on caissons, and at least five are on fort walls." Michigan is home to about one-hundred- twenty-four lighthouses.
Photography by Shangle Photographics

Statue of George Armstrong Custer, Monroe

Monroe boasts of a Civil War hero, George Armstrong Custer, who called Monroe home before his military service began. Constructed in 1920 the bronze statue titled "Sighting the Enemy" was dedicated to the memory of their hero and resident. Monroe is home to the Monroe County Historical Society and the River Raisin Battlefield Visitor Center. Both facilities provide in-depth information regarding the area history. *Photography by Shangle Photographics*

Grand Haven boat harbor, southwestern Michigan on Lake Michigan

Visit Grand Haven to experience a real summer resort town. "So much to do and so little time to do it" seems to linger on the minds of eager vacation visitors. Anytime is a good time at Grand Haven, touted to be one of Western Michigan's most popular resort areas, and it is extremely colorful during the Kite Festival in May. There is a riverboat cruise to take, leisure pleasure-craft boating on the Lake, and delightful shopping areas for those curio and souvenir seekers. The Gillette Sand Dune Visitor Center provides mounds of information regarding natures wildlife and Grand Haven is very proud of the World's Largest Musical Fountain.

Photography by James Blank

Lower Falls, Tehquamenon Falls State Park

The wide spreading river cascades around an island creating the Lower Falls of the Tehquamenon, located on the Upper Peninsula in Tehquamenon Falls State Park in Hiawatha National Forest. Unique in that the waterfalls are five separate cascading units, the tumbling amber water of the river is caused by tannin leached from Cedar, Hemlock and Spruce trees. The romantic prose of Henry Wadsworth Longfellow's *Song of Hiawatha* refers to the rushing river, the singing birds and the "solitary forest" found here in Tehquamenon Falls State Park. Rich in lore and rich in amenities, the park provides opportunities for hiking, canoeing, camping and exploring nature to its fullest. Birds are plentiful. Wildlife such as Black bear, coyotes, deer, beaver and mink make their home in the area. When winter arrives to the area, access is still possible to the year-around-park and there is a great opportunity for cross-country skiing, snowmobiling and snowshoe hiking. *Photography by Shangle Photographics*

Henry Ford Museum, Dearborn

Born on July 30, 1863, in Dearborn, Henry Ford was one of six children born to William and Mary Ford. Farming was a way of life for most people in Dearborn but Henry preferred tinkering with machinery and disliked farming. It was this natural interest in mechanical things that caused Henry Ford to pursue his desire to invent. The Henry Ford Museum documents the history of transportation through technology.

Photography by Shangle Photographics

Mackinac Bridge, Mackinaw City, Straits of Mackinac

Mackinac Bridge is one of the longest suspension bridges in the world, a five-mile span. Until its completion in 1957, a passenger and car ferry served the Upper and Lower peninsulas. Those long lines of automobiles waiting for their turn to take passage on the ferry have been eliminated. An annual event held in September on Labor Day is the Bridge Walk, the only day that foot-traffic can use the bridge. Over 60,000 walkers participate, walking between Mackinaw City on the Lower Peninsula and St. Ignace on the Upper Peninsula.

Photography by Shangle Photographics

Copper Harbor on Keweenaw Peninsula, Lake Superior

This Upper Peninsula village is the northernmost community in Michigan and the anchor of the Copper Heritage. Would-be copper miners inhabited Copper Harbor soon after a huge pure-veined copper deposit was discovered in 1843. With its excellent harbor and easy access by Lake Freighters, Copper Harbor became a shipping and receiving port on Lake Superior. Once the copper industry was the economic lifeline for the area, while today tourism is the primary source of economic stability. Visitors can tour the peninsula and take in the 1849 Copper Harbor Lighthouse and investigate local history at the Museum. Historic Fort Wilkins reveals garrisoned life at the early military post built to maintain civility in the area. Isle Royale is just a short boat trip away. *Photography by Shangle Photographics*

Eagle Harbor Lighthouse, Eagle Harbor, Keweenaw Peninsula

Maintained by the United States Coast Guard, this historical operating lighthouse, first built in 1851 as a wooden tower then reconstructed in 1871 to a larger structure, is now a museum as well as being an active lighthouse. The Keweenaw County Historical Society has jurisdiction over the museum. Along with the lighthouse there is the 1871 light keepers home, and there are shipwreck artifacts that illustrate the harrowing life of early sailors on Lake Superior. Eagle Harbor is located in the north-central section of the Keweenaw Peninsula along Lake Superior on the Upper Peninsula.

Photography by Shangle Photographics

West of Jackson on Interstate Highway 94 is Battle Creek. The name of Kellogg and Battle Creek always go together in Michigan, as do corn flakes and cereal. The Kellogg brothers developed the flake cereal at Battle Creek and the rest of the story is history. You can see that history come alive at Kellogg's Cereal City USA, "a themed family attraction." The Mission Statement is "To be a Historical and Educational Facility that conveys the Development, Growth, and Global Impact of the Cereal Industry in a Fun, Entertaining, and Interactive manner." Battle Creek has a great deal of history and shares it. The Kellogg House is located in downtown Battle Creek at Linear Park, next to the Community Flower Garden. The "Leila Arboretum Society in partnership with the W. K. Kellogg Foundation" developed and currently maintains the Garden, which displays over 3,000 trees and shrubs. There are gardens specifically designed to display floral colors as the season changes. A monument honoring Harriet Tubman and Erastus and Sarah Hussey is also located in Linear Park. These people voluntarily exposed themselves to danger by secretly moving runaway slaves in the 1840s and 1850s to safe havens. Slaves of the south were doing their best to flee to a place of freedom, where a life of oppression and fear would leave them. The Underground Railroad Sculpture pays honor to the courage and the achievements of the people involved and to those who moved over 1,000 people to a safer life. The Binder Park Zoo and the Leila Arboretum are also two special places to visit.

A few miles west is the city of Kalamazoo, home to many of the "Who's-Who" national corporations that give an economic base to the area. Things to see and things to do in Kalamazoo are many. There is a choice of the Kalamazoo Valley Museum, the Nature Center, Air Zoo, the Gilmore-Classic Car Club of America Museum, and many more attractions. Lake Michigan is just a short drive west where excellent beaches provide an opportunity for fishing, swimming, kite flying and for creating an old fashioned sand castle. The winter sports of skiing and skating are not to be overlook either. There is alpine skiing north at Ostego, northwest at Govels and south at Three Rivers, just north of U.S. 12.

There are excellent cross-country ski locations in the vicinity, as well as lakes for skating and areas designated for tobogganing and snow tubing.

Kalamazoo began in the late 1700s as a small fur-trading post. It was in 1829 that Titus Bronson, who is credited as the city's founder, arrived and he is remembered by having Bronson Park named in his honor. The city provides an opportunity to experience art, entertainment and history. The 750-acre campus of Western Michigan University is here, along with Kalamazoo College and several other centers of higher learning.

South of Kalamazoo is an important suburb known as Portage. It was first settled in 1830 and its original name was Sweetland. That name didn't last long, for in 1838 the town was renamed for Portage Creek.

All of the small towns along U.S. 12 and I-94 have individual history and importance. These towns are the true foundation of the area. The village of Saline incorporated in 1866 but began long before in 1826. Mr. Orange Risdon surveyed Saline village in 1832 and is credited as the town's founder. Visit Saline during its annual Celtic Festival. Jonesville was the first registered community in Hillsdale County, established in 1828 by Beniah Jones. Headwaters of the St. Joseph River flow here. South on State Highway 99 is the town of Hillsdale, first settled in 1834 by Jeremiah Arnold and the home to Michigan's first coeducational parochial college established in 1844, Hillsdale College. Coldwater was first established in 1833 and took its name from the creek that runs through town. Tourism and cultural activities play a big part in the economic structure in the town. A must-see item is the historical Tibbits Opera House. The town of Sturgis, named for Judge John Sturgis, was incorporated as a village in 1855 and as a city in 1986. White Pigeon was incorporated in 1837, making it the oldest incorporated village in Michigan. White Pigeon is named for an Indian chief. Thomas H. Edwards founded Edwardsburg in 1828 but it wasn't until 1911 that the village incorporated. Further west is Niles, the "City of Four Flags." Niles is proud of its extensive history, dating back as far as 1680 when Jesuit missionaries established a mission they named St. Joseph de la Miami. Through the days of the French and Indian War and the American Revolution, up through the time when the village was named for Hezekiah Niles in 1829, Niles' history has been colored by England, France, Spain and the United States. The town is quite proud of its famous people such as Aaron Montgomery Ward, Dr. F. N. Bonine, famous ophthalmologist and four-time mayor, and John and Horace Dodge, founders of the Dodge Brothers Company. The Fort St. Joseph Museum provides an extensive historic interpretation of the area.

The town of Berrien Springs is on U.S. Highway 31 northwest of Niles. It began as Wolf's Prairie, named for a local Indian chief. But in 1831 the name was changed to Berrien, honoring John M. Berrien, Attorney General of the United States during the administration of President Andrew Jackson. At the time of incorporation in 1863, the name *Springs* was added to reflect the numerous natural springs found in the area. Andrews University is located here, "a Christian university in the Seventh-day Adventist tradition."

Along Interstate Highway 94 is the town of Paw Paw, a village that "retains the quaint friendly atmosphere of a rural farm community combined with modern shops and market facilities." Seventeenth-century Jesuit missionaries named the river after the Paw Paw fruit tree that grew wild in the river bottom land. The settlement then took its name from the river in 1838. Two small towns to the west are Lawrence and Hartford. Both towns are involved in light manufacturing and agriculture.

Life is a little different when you find yourself at Lake Michigan. There is much more tourism, which can speed up one's way of life, and there are different things to do for fun. There certainly is an abundance of lake front property and small towns to explore.

At the most southern edge of Michigan along the lake are two very small resort towns, Michiana and Grand Beach. New Buffalo, located on the Galien River, was there first in 1836 when it was incorporated as a city. There are several quaint resort towns north, Union Pier, Lakeside, Harbert and Chikaming Township. A must-see place is Warren Dunes State Park, a 1,950-acre park that has sand dunes that rise 240 feet. It is a great place to explore. There are six miles of ski and toboggan trails. Adjacent to the park is the

Warren Woods Nature Center. When autumn colors set on the trees, here is a place to visit. Camping and picnic facilities are available at both parks.

Bridgman was first known as Plummer's Pier and also as Charlotte. It became Bridgman in 1874. Pass through Stevensville and Shoreham, primarily residential communities, and enter the bustling towns of St. Joseph and Benton Harbor, where the St. Joseph River empties into Lake Michigan. The St. Joseph Lighthouse guards the harbor of this deep-water port. The lighthouse became quite popular when the United States Government printed its image on a commemorative postage stamp. Rightfully so, its grandeur enhances the area along the shoreline known as "The Riviera of the Midwest."

Southwest Michigan is the center for peach orchards. The first peach tree planted in Michigan was here in the 1780s by William Burnett. A plentiful crop is grown, giving Michigan a rank of sixth in the nation for growing peaches. A Peach Festival is held annually Coloma, north of St. Joseph, in midsummer.

Interstate 96, which parallels the Lake Michigan shoreline, has many exit points for the traveler who would like to take excursions away from the fast pace of the freeway. South Haven proclaims to be the Blueberry Capital of the World. Agriculture, manufacturing and tourism give the economic boost to South Haven.

The Kalamazoo River divides the two towns of Douglas and Saugatuck: Douglas is on the south side and Saugatuck is on the north side. Once it was necessary to take a chain-powered ferry across the river. Now a bridge connects the towns. Cruise boats are available for river and lake excursions at Douglas and Saugatuck. The *SS Keewatin* is a classic steamship museum moored near Douglas. Saugatuck also has a longtime reputation as an art colony.

A visit to Holland is a cherished experience. Anytime is a *great* time to visit Holland, but especially in mid-May when thousands of tulips are in bloom. It is Tulip Time, the annual celebration of Dutch Heritage, which began to take shape in 1926 as a dream. The dream became a reality in 1928 when

100,000 tulip bulbs arrived from Netherlands and were planted by the citizens. The following May the Tulip Time festival began and it has been a constant event ever since, save a few years during World War II. Windmill Island Park has a working Dutch Windmill well over 200-years old, an antique carousel and a 17th-century Dutch country store, and many more interesting and historical items available.

East of Holland is a place that commands an audience and that place is Grand Rapids, located on the banks of the Grand River. The river adds a certain dimension to the city one needs to experience. Capitalizing on waterpower and the plentiful timber in the forests, Grand Rapids developed a commanding position in furniture manufacturing, and it still holds the honor. The Frederik Meijer Gardens, the Van Andel Museum and the Gerald R. Ford Museum, honoring the nation's 38th President, are fine examples of attractions Grand Rapids provides for the visitor and its people.

Back along the lake is Grand Haven, Spring Lake and Ferrysburg: the Tri-Cities of Michigan. This truly is a resort area. There are spectacular swimming beaches; beautiful sand dunes, where a vehicle can be hired for sand dune rides; a marina for boating and fishing, and lots of specialty shops. Near the waterfront boardwalk at Grand Haven is a 10,000-square-foot wooden playground that an entire family can enjoy.

The name Muskegon has a curious sound. It "is derived from the Ottawa Indian term *'Mosqugon'* meaning 'marshy river or swamp'." A trading post took shape between 1790 and 1800 at the mouth of Duck Lake. However, it was 1837 when the township was organized. Lumber was the prime source for Muskegon's existence, providing the title Lumber Queen of the World. Times changed and diversification was mandated. Muskegon has stood tall through the economic challenge. Today, manufacturing and tourism are two strong economic supports for the city and surrounding area, along with cultural and recreation activities. Muskegon is the largest city in western Michigan. A family city it is, proud of its community strength and open-arm policy to visitors.

Ludington is a welcomed sight for those "shortcut takers" who need to get to Wisconsin. Seasonal ferry service is available here on the *SS Badger*. Service began in 1992. There are so many things to experience in Ludington and the surrounding area. When weather permits, investigate the catamaran rides and antique boats; do some charter fishing for salmon and trout; there are plenty of camping facilities too. Wintertime sports include cross-country skiing and snowmobiling.

Manistee is a charming village thirty-one-miles north of Ludington. Restoring its historic district that parallels the Manistee River has authenticated the expression "The Victorian Port City." "The Manistee Fire Hall, built in 1888, is the oldest continuously active fire station in Manistee" and it adds to the distinction of being a National Historic District. The Riverwalk extends 1.5-miles from the U.S. Highway 31 bridge to the sand dunes of Lake Michigan.

A point of interest. East of Manistee is the town of Cadillac. Where did it get its name? Not from the car. It was named for Antoine de la Mothe Cadillac, the founder of Detroit.

West of U.S. 31 off Benzie County Road 115 is Frankfort, where fishing is exceptional and Michigan beauty excels. A wooden cross and marker indicate the place where it is believed the Jesuit priest, Jacques Marquette, died in 1675, at the mouth of the Betsie Bay.

Frankfort is at the southern entrance to Sleeping Bear Dunes National Lakeshore that consists of thirty-five-miles of shoreline northward, along the northwest Lake Michigan shoreline. There are two islands offshore known as the North and South Manitou island that are part of the national Lakeshore. A Native American story tells of a mother bear and her two cubs that swam across Lake Michigan toward the Michigan shore to escape danger. Only the mother bear was able to complete the crossing, while the two cubs were lost to the water. The cubs have been immortalized as North and South Manitou islands. The mother made it to shore and climbed to the top of the dunes where she rested and waited for her cubs. Hence, "The Sleeping Bear." It is an Ojibway Indian story. The National Shoreline provides exceptional scenic drives and miles of shoreline fun. There are fifty-five miles of marked trails for hiking and cross-country skiing. Passenger ferry service is available to the island, where hiking and backpacking opens new vistas. A visitor center is at Empire, near mid-park, which exhibits materials regarding the natural history of the area. Just west of Glen Haven is the Maritime Museum that provides in-depth marine history.

It is now a proper time to reflect on Michigan's Wine Country. Leelanau Peninsula stretches north, along with Old Mission Peninsula, and this is one of the wine-producing sections in Michigan, specifically Michigan's Northwest Wine Country. The other major wine area is in the southwest section of Michigan, from Union Pier north to Muskegon and up to and east towards Kalamazoo and Grand Rapids. Growing conditions for grapes are excellent. Since the late 1960s, an increase in the varieties of grapes has been introduced to the many vineyards. It is a growing business and Michigan stands tall in the wine industry.

Traverse City, founded in 1891 at the southern terminus of Grand Traverse Bay, has a real hold on the activities in the area. Boating and fishing are outstanding in the bay. Vacation resorts are numerous and tourism flourishes. Agriculturally speaking, Traverse City carries the title Cherry Capital of the World. Every summer a great cherry festival is held in Traverse City.

Don't miss the scenic drive on Old Mission Peninsula before continuing the trip north on U.S. 31 to Charlevoix, a small resort town on the west end of beautiful Lake Charlevoix and on the eastern shore of Lake Michigan. There is ferry service from Charlevoix to Beaver Island located about thirty-miles west in Lake Michigan. The island was first occupied by the French but abandoned in 1603; a self-appointed king, James Jesse Strang, a leader to a group of settling Mormons in 1847, then occupied it. The colony was forced to abandon their holding in 1856. Eventually, Irish immigrants established a fishing settlement. Today the island is a haven for vacation seekers.

It is a pretty drive to Petosky, a small town in the heart of the vacation land located on Little Traverse Bay. Petosky State Park is a paradise for rock hounds, who forage the beach for the elusive Petosky stone, the Michigan state stone since 1965. On the north side of Little Traverse Bay is Harbor Springs, a quiet, relaxed area that is well groomed and a reverse of bustling Petosky and points south.

Small communities dot the landscape toward the Straits of Mackinac and Mackinaw City. Locate For Michilimackinac, a twenty-seven acre historic attraction known as Colonial Michilimackinac. The British occupied the French-built fort (1715) from 1761 to 1781.

The famous Mackinac Bridge dominates the landscape and is one of the most appreciated sights around, connecting the Lower and Upper peninsulas. It is one of the longest suspension bridges in the world, a five-mile span. Until its completion in 1957, a passenger and car ferry served the peninsulas. Those long, lines of automobiles waiting for their turn to take passage on the ferry have been eliminated. The official first crossing day was November 1, 1957. An annual event since 1958, when at that time there were only sixty participants, is the Labor Day Bridge Walk, the only day that foot-traffic can use the bridge. Now there are well over 60,000 walkers participating in this special event, walking between Mackinac City and St. Ignance on the Upper Peninsula. An item to use in the next trivia game is to know that there are some "42,000 miles of cable that spans the length of the bridge." Summer and winter, Mackinaw City is a special place.

Read most any vacation guide and it will refer to Michigan's Crown Jewel, Mackinac Island, where living is quiet, serene and slow paced. Unless someone is ill and needs an ambulance or there is a fire and the police and fire equipment are needed, the only mode of transportation while on the island is by horse-drawn carriage, bicycle or horseback, or the tried-and-true method of walking. The island, only three-miles long and two-miles wide, has interesting terrain of ravines, caves and quizzical rock formations. Special scenic locations are Arch Rock, Sugar Loaf and Mackinac Island State Park. There are several sites that are most important in order to understand the historical significance of the area. Fort Mackinac is a restored 18th- and

19th-century military outpost, now serving as an interpretive museum. And there is the historic Grand Hotel, itself a prominent fixture in the island's community. Access to the island is by ferryboat, from Mackinaw City or St. Ignace. The racing water of the Straits of Mackinac pour between Lakes Michigan on the west into Huron on the east, which is home to Mackinac Island.

Most of the towns located on the eastern half of the Lower Peninsula came about during the lumber years, in the 1880s. The rivers were used to float the timber out to Lake Huron where it was loaded onto ships, causing some towns to develop into major shipping ports. Cheyboygan, a Chippewa Indian word that translates to "Water of the Chippewas", flourished as a port town. Today it is deeply involved with tourism, commercial fishing, some farming and limestone. Its neighbor, Rogers City, contains the largest limestone quarry in the world, causing it to be a major port of call for Great Lake freighters.

Out from Rogers City to the west are small towns that make a strong mark on Michigan's economy and history. The town of Onaway on SR 68 and 33 grew during the lumber era. It was first settled in 1880. Big Black Lake is north of Onaway, once the fishing center for sturgeon. Sturgeon is still caught in Black Lake and Onaway is still known as the Sturgeon Capital of Michigan.

South on State Road 33 is Atlanta, county seat of Montmorency County. Thunder Bay River State Forest is here and very large herds of elk, numbering about 500 to 600 in total, call the forest home. Because of the elk grazing about Atlanta, the town has become known as the "Elk Capital of Michigan." There are many lakes in the central-eastern section of Michigan that give rise to year 'round fishing, and summer boating and swimming. Thunder Bay River flows through the landscape gathering tributaries as it moves along before emptying into Thunder Bay. For want of something to do that is a little different, take time to explore Thunder Bay, underwater, and view the shipwreck sites that provide an interesting explore opportunity. Dated back to 1848, the vessel *New Orleans* ran aground in heavy fog while carrying passengers. There are sunken ships that allow divers an opportunity to snoop.

The city of Alpena is located on Thunder Bay, the largest industrial city in Alpena County. Farming is important in this area, producing potatoes, winter wheat, oats and strawberries. Dairy herds, cattle ranching, limestone mining and fishing still prove to be strong economic factors here. Presque Isle, just north on Lake Huron, "continues to top the list for big game fishermen, ranking as the state's best Chinook salmon fishery." Presque Isle County has plenty of game birds for the hunter and plenty of play ground for skiers and snowmobiles. Each summer the Classic Wooden Boat Show is held along with the Nautical Festival. South into Alcona and Oscoda counties there are several lakes and rivers that provide respite for the weary who need relaxation and a departure from the fast pace of life. Hubbard Lake is one of Michigan's largest lakes.

Towering white-pine forests once stood in this vast area, drawing lumbermen who made a fortune from the industry. The Huron-Manistee National Forest spreads across the state "created from abandoned farms and lumbered wastelands that were unwanted." National Forest information states that there are a total of 964,413 acres in the forestlands, of which 5,786 acres are wetland. The Huron National Forest is in the northeastern part of lower-Michigan and the Manistee National Forest is in the western part. The two forests were combined in 1945.

The River Road Scenic Byway, a twenty-two mile paved highway, has been established in the Huron National Forest along the scenic Au Sable River. The Lumbermen's Monument is here, which pays tribute to the lumber era of the late 1800s. The waters of the Au Sable have been tamed by a series of dams used to produce power and to develop a fine recreation environment. Those who enjoy paddling a canoe can paddle for miles in the waters of the Au Sable. A Canoe Memorial has been erected honoring those "who traversed the Au Sable." Annually, the Au Sable River Run has canoeists paddling from Grayling, mid-state, out to Oscoda ,where the river enters Lake Huron.

South on U.S. 23 are Tawas City, East Tawas and Tawas Point, named for a local Ottawa Indian chief, Otawas. From Tawas City west off SR 55 are

West Branch, Prudenville and Houghton Lake, one of Michigan's vacation wonderlands. The lake is the state's "largest body of inland water, and the source of the Muskegon River." Higgins Lakes, north and Houghton Lake are summer and winter recreational sites.

Montcalm County, south of Mecosta County is recognized as an agricultural area growing primarily potatoes. With the many lakes scattered throughout the area, tourism is an important economic factor. The towns of Greenville and Stanton are the largest in the county. Stanton maintains a well-groomed, old-fashioned 1900s appearance and exemplifies the quaintness during the annual Old Fashioned Days festival held in August. In 1840 the town was called Fred. When the town incorporated as a village in 1863, the name was changed to Stanton, honoring Edwin M. Stanton, Secretary of War during Lincoln's administration. Greenville is the commercial leader in the county, utilizing manufacturing as an economic stabilizer. August is a busy month in Montcalm county as Greenville celebrates its Danish Festival.

Take State Highway 57 east through small farmland areas, then north on U.S. 27 to the county seat of Gratiot County, Ithaca. Retaining its historical significance is important to Ithaca and the handsome courthouse and Fire Hall are evidence of that pride. If you want to be in the center of things, go north to St. Louis, which "occupies the exact geographical center of Michigan's Lower Peninsula." East of St. Louis is the city of Saginaw, county seat of Saginaw County, located in the heart of Saginaw Valley.

Bay City has been in existence since the 1830s when Leon Trombley chose to keep his horse rather than swap for the swampland that is now home to Bay City. That Swampland is a major industrial and agricultural distribution center on Lake Huron. BayCityOnLine states, "More waterborne tonnage is handled at the Bay City Port area than at any of the 31 other Michigan port cities, excluding Detroit." Several other industries add to the economic strength of the area, namely automotive parts, industrial manufacturing and agriculture, specifically sugar beets and beans.

U.S. Highway 23 leads the way to one of the most visited cities in Michigan, Frankenmuth, a German settlement with roots back to the 1840s. The town center is old Bavaria, with gingerbread trim and laced with nostalgia. Keeping a spirit of festivity, take time to enjoy the week long Bavarian Fest in June, and the annual Octoberfest. Actually, Frankenmuth has special-interest activities year 'round, either sponsored by the entire community or by private business. Frankenmuth is truly a tourist-holiday town, and if Christmas is a favorite holiday, you are in luck. The world's largest Christmas store is here in Frankenmuth, Bronner's Christmas Wonderland.

About thirty-miles south is the city of Flint, one of the automotive centers of Michigan and the birthplace of General Motors. Before cars were invented, horse-drawn carriages were the mode of transportation, and carriage manufacturing was a big item in Flint. Visit the Alfred P. Sloan Museum for a complete history of General Motors, beginning with history of William "Billly" Durant, founder of General Motors. Become involved with the accomplishments of the late Alfred P. Sloan, who worked his way through the ranks at General Motors to become President and then Chairman-of-the-Board. Flint provides the Flint Cultural Center, Institute of Art, and the Longway Planetarium. East of town is a natural outdoor setting known as the Genesee Recreation Area where folks can linger away time and enjoy boating, fishing, hiking, camping and the old-fashioned picnic.

Between Flint and Port Huron is furtive farmland. Towns such as Davison, Lapeer and Imlay City serve the people in the farmland communities. Now is an excellent opportunity to go north and investigate the *Thumb* of Michigan's mitten. Imlay City is referred to by some as the Gateway to the Thumb. State Road 53 extends to the most northern point, Port Austin, where "the sun rises and sets on the water." Follow State Road 245 west to Caseville, located on Saginaw Bay, where windsurfing has become an exciting sport. Caseville is famous for fishing, boating, and as a great vacation spot. South is Sebewaing, a small town with a big marina for boaters and fishermen. Tourism definitely plays a big part of Sebewaing's economy but so do sugar beets. The Thumb area grows a lot of sugar beets, and Sebewaing is home to Michigan

Sugar Company. Sugar beets are processed here as well as in Carrollton, near Saginaw, Bay City, Caro and Croswell, east of Sandusky and west of Port Sanilac, an historic waterfront village on the shore of Lake Huron. Sebewaing has an annual Sugar Festival. Sugar and Fun are two big items available on the Thumb. Another big item is "the world's largest man-made fresh water harbor" at Harbor Beach, east and south of Port Austin. There are several county parks on the lakeshore that provide camping facilities, hiking and cross-country ski trails. For those looking for more refined lodging, Harbor Beach can provide that, along with a place to quench the browsing urge in the downtown area. South along Highway 25 is the small town of Lexington, "the first settlement on the shore of Lake Huron north of Port Huron."

Lake Huron has provided livelihood for people since the early 1800s and it still does. Fishing and boating opportunities lead to great tourism and commercial industries for all of the communities near the lake. Lake Huron is the second largest of the Great Lakes, covering 23,010-square-miles. Also, it is the fourth largest lake in the world. Water passes from Lake Superior into Lake Huron through the St. Marys River at Sault Ste. Marie and from Lake Huron into Lake Erie through the St. Clair River that drains into St. Clair Lake. The lake water then flows into the Detroit River, which goes into Lake Erie.

Highway 24 leads to Port Huron located on the St. Clair River and Lake Huron. Interstate Highway 94 aims towards Detroit, the largest city in Michigan. Many important communities create Detroit's superstructure, making it economically strong. Some of the cities around Detroit were created by urban sprawl and are relatively new to the scene, such as Southfield, incorporating into a city structure in 1958. The city of Livonia in 1996 "was rated in the top ten cities in the country in which to raise a family." Pontiac, a national leader in the automotive industry, is the county seat to Oakland County. The city of Troy is the twelfth largest city in Michigan.

All of the communities around Detroit are an integral part of the whole, making Detroit bigger than it really is. Its location along the twenty-seven mile Detroit River was important back in 1701 when French trappers and explorers settled in the area, just as it is important today. When the automobile came to Detroit, it changed everything for the city. Industry growth demanded people to work in the factories, and with the influx of people, support businesses increased. A population explosion was the result.

Today, Detorit is known as *the automotive center* of the world. The cities of Dearborn, Pontiac and Auburn Hills are considered by many, primarily outsiders, as Detroit. But there is more to Detroit. The Detroit/Wayne County Port Authority really says it best. "Internationally known for automobile manufacturing and trade, the world headquarters for General Motors Corp., Ford Motor Co., Daimler-Chrysler, and Volkswagen of America are located in Metropolitan Detroit. The area ranks as a leader in the production of paints, non-electrical machinery, automation equipment, pharmaceuticals, rubber products, synthetic resins, and garden seed. National and international corporations headquartered here include Kmart, The Budd Company, Stroh's Brewery Company, American National Resources and Federal Mogul. These companies help employ more than two-million metro Detroiters." Two-airport terminals service the area: Detroit Wayne County Metropolitan Airport and Detroit City Airport.

Take time to investigate the bright spots in Detroit. There are many museums of all kinds available. There is the Charles H. Wright Museum of African American History, Detroit's Historical Museum, Institute of Arts and Science Center. Visit the Motown Historical Museum and the Old Mariners Church. Take in an athletic event, experiencing professional baseball, football and hockey. These are always exciting. History dominates the area for miles around, so spend some time viewing the historical sites.

South past Wayne County is the only county located along Lake Erie, Monroe County. Agriculture leads the way here, along with "auto-parts manufacturing, metal fabrication, cement, packaging, and glass production." The towns along the Erie shore all have shallow, marshy land that appeals to wildlife, especially birds. Fishing is good as well as boating.

The town of South Rockwood is primarily a residential community and a Detroit suburb. Estral Beach borders Swan Creek and is a summer resort settlement along Lake Erie. The city of Monroe is the large center for activity in Monroe County and is the primary service center for the small communities. The French came to this part of Michigan in 1780 and settled here along the north side of the Raisin River in what became known as Frenchtown. The Americans settled on the south side of the river in 1817 and named their town Monroe, after the fifth president of the United States, James Monroe. Monroe boasts of a Civil War hero who called Monroe home, George Armstrong Custer. The Monroe County Historical Museum provides an in-depth interpretation to the rich history of Monroe and the surrounding area. The River Raisin Battlefield Visitor Center is a wonderful place to learn about the intense battle referred to as the River Raisin Massacre, fought in Monroe in 1813 during the War of 1812.

The resort town of Luna Pier and Erie, south of Monroe, provide a quick getaway from Toledo, Ohio, These towns are just a few mile north of one of Ohio's largest cities.

West of Monroe are the towns of Dundee, Blissfield, Tecumseh and Adrian. Adrian is the largest of the towns and is the county seat of Lenawee County. Adrian displays an historic downtown area that can easily represent the early development of the surrounding lands. The historic significance has been maintained in much of its architecture. The county's name, Lenawee, is a Shawnee word for Indian.

Lenawee County is where this trip through the Lower Peninsula began, several pages back. As a reminder to yourself, visit the scenic Irish Hills, again, and reminisce about all the lovely places you have been to in Michigan.

Upper Peninsula

Crossing the Mackinac Bridge to the Upper Peninsula is like opening the first page of a second volume in a book series. The first volume was so good that a second volume was necessary to write. Of course, the second volume has its own identity and stands on its own merits. That is the way the Upper Peninsula of Michigan is to be considered. It stands on its own merits and is exciting for what it offers.

Start with St. Ignace, one of the oldest towns in Michigan, located on the southern edge of the peninsula on the Straits of Mackinac. Jesuit priest Jacques Marquette established a mission in 1671 and the military made itself present soon after. Within 30 years both the mission and the military abandoned the site.

Interstate Highway 75 spans north between Hiawatha National Forest and Superior State Forest, lands set aside by the government for safekeeping. It is a fifty-two-mile road trip to Sault Ste. Marie, the third oldest continuous settlement in the United States. French fur traders were the first to establish the area, which they called Sault du Gaustogne. In 1688 Jesuit priests, Jacques Marquette and Claude Dablon, arrived and established a mission, changing the name of the settlement to Sault. Ste. Marie in honor of the Virgin Mary.

Today Sault Ste. Marie's primary job is tending the boat locks on the St. Marys River. There are other activities the city is involved with but the locks are the most impressionable. Lock operations allow lake traffic to navigate over rapids that create a twenty-one-foot variance between Lakes Superior and Huron. There are four locks, referred to as the Soo Locks. The first of the locks was built in 1844. (The very first lock was built on the Canadian side of the river in 1797 and was destroyed in the War of 1812.) Today the four Soo locks, located in the St. Mary Falls Canal, create the world's largest locking system. Sault Ste. Marie, Michigan, and Sault Ste. Marie, Ontario, Canada, are linked via highway and railroad bridge. Sault Ste. Marie is a port-of-entry to Canada.

There are many things to see and places to go in Sault Ste. Marie. Tours on boats and trains provide excellent exploring of the Soo Locks along with extensive visual and verbal explanations. The history of the St. Marys River and its environs is available at the River of History Museum. The Visitor's Bureau says, "There is a debate about what the name translates to, but French speakers say "Sault" means "to jump," making Sault St. Marie the place where people would come to "jump the St. Marys."

State Road 28 is the primary road, passing through the entire length of the Peninsula, east to west, and intersecting with several roads that lead to particularly beautiful locations. One such intersection is State Highway 123, leading north to Tahquamenon Falls State Park, the Land of Hiawatha. Primarily undeveloped woodland, the park consists of nearly 40,000 acres. There are two main waterfalls on the Tahquamenon River. Capturing the record as the largest waterfall east of the Mississippi River, the Upper Falls drops nearly 50 feet and spans over 200 feet. The Lower Falls is actually five smaller falls spread across the width of the river flowing around an island but they are accepted as one total unit. The river's headwater is north of McMillan and travels about ninety-five miles to Whitefish Bay in Lake Superior.

Highway 123 goes on to Newberry, south, and to the intersection of State Highway 77, where the road north touches the southern edge of Lake Superior at Grand Marias and Au Sable Point. Here is the eastern edge of

Pictured Rocks National Shoreline, extending forty miles west of Munising. There are two information centers, Munising Falls Interpretive Center near Sand Point and Grand Sable Visitor Center, west of Grand Marias. There is information regarding the summer activities of boating, swimming, hiking and backpacking, and winter activities regarding cross-country ski trails, snowshoeing, ice fishing and requirements and restrictions regarding snowmobiling. Cliffs along the shoreline reach heights of two-hundred feet.

Munising is at the western edge of Pictured Rocks off Trout Bay on Lake Superior. Grand Island, a National Recreation Area, is located in the bay and acts as a buffer against winds blowing in off of the lake that can reach gale force. In its own right, Grand Island is a world of its own. Not a huge island but the largest of the islands on Lake Superior's south shore; it provides thirty-five miles of shoreline that encircles some 13,500 acres of dense hardwood forest. The island is about eight-miles long and three-miles wide. Campsites are available, but bring your own drinking water. Spend time here enjoying the pristine beauty and the more primitive environs. The Ojibway Indians made Grand Island their home. Ferry service is available between Munising and Grand Island. In winter the hum of the snowmobile can be heard with regularity in Munising, which is known as the Snowmobiling Capital of the World. There are some 250 lakes in the area, making it ideal for fishing and canoeing.

The city of Marquette, nestled in the Laurentian Uplands on the southern shores of Lake Superior, began as a shipping center. The city was named for Father Jacques Marquette, French missionary and explorer who came to the Michigan Territory in the latter part of the 1600s. Marquette is home to Northern Michigan University and Presque Isle Park, an excellent summer and winter park. There are several museums that provide historical information about the area. The Marquette Maritime Museum features maritime heritage of Marquette and Lake Superior. Marquette is the service center for the western portion of the Upper Peninsula.

West are the town of Negaunee and Ishpeming, each becoming cities in 1873, and both are iron ore communities. The Jackson Iron Company first settled Negaunee in 1846. Ten years later, in 1857, Ishpeming was established and referred to as Lake Superior Location. That name was not specific enough for a postal location so the name Ishpeming was chosen. (*Ishpeming* is a Chippewa Indian word for "a high place.")

A most interesting place to visit is McCormick Wilderness, 16,850 acres of wetlands created by eighteen small lakes, numerous swamp areas and the Yellow Dog River that is designated a National Wild and Scenic River. This parcel of land was donated to the state in 1967 by the McCormick family, the estate of Gordon McCormick, and a descendant of Cyrus H. McCormick, inventor of the reaping machine.

West on U.S. 41 is an area of many lakes, from the very small to the very large, most of them natural lakes. One of the lakes along the highway is Lake Michigamme, a real big wilderness lake covering 4,360 acres and reaching depths of over fifty feet. Take a boat and explore the more than twenty islands located within the lake, or go fishing for the elusive muskie, or for Northern pike, Walleye, Small-mouth bass, and perch.

Lakes in the western section of the Upper Peninsula are in the hundreds, most all of them accessible for fishing. Some lakes are naturally more popular than others but if a stand is taken on which one is the most popular, a heated discussion will ensue and everybody will be right. The big ones are always safe in mentioning, like Michigamme Reservoir, Peavy Pond, Lac Vieux Desert, Lake Gogebic and the famous Cisco Chain of Lakes south of Watersmeet. This lake area is Moose Country and it is feasible to see the moose here as well as other wild creatures such as Red fox, deer, Black bear, maybe a wolf and the inevitable raccoon.

North on L'Anse Bay are two small communities, namely Baraga and L'Anse, both locations sharing kinship to the early trappers and the American Fur Company identified with John Jacob Astor. Names associated with the area are John Sunday, a Chippewa Indian who took his Christian name when he converted to a Methodist belief, and Jesuit priests René Menard and Claude Allouer. There was Peter Crebassa who got Father Baraga to come to the area. Captain James Bendry is recognized as the founder of Baraga. For the stout of heart, venture east of L'Anse to Mt. Arvon, elevation 1,979 feet, and the highest point in Michigan.

North of Baraga is Chassell, receiving its name from John Chassell the area's first settler. John sold his holding to Sturgeon River Lumber Company who built a sawmill and developed the town site in 1881. Beyond are two towns most important to the area, Hancock and Houghton, located along Portage Lake. Copper was the driving force for the development of the towns, until the mining industry waned due to low prices and the high cost for production. Since diversification was necessary for a continued existence, Houghton took the rein of ingenuity and brought about a change that placed it into an economic upward spiral. Houghton has the advantage of being at the entrance to Keweenaw Peninsula, which has developed along with Houghton as a tourist center. Outdoor activities beckon the would-be adventurer from many parts of Michigan and beyond. Excellent water sports, fishing, hiking and camping are available for fair weather times; winter sports that include cross-country and downhill skiing and ice fishing. And Houghton has a Winter Carnival that brings out the artist flair of people that must be enjoyed. And of course, there are many historical attractions in the Houghton and Hancock area that need viewing.

To have communities on each side of Portage Lake Canal created a problem of crossing to the other side. A steam ferry was first implemented, followed by a wooden bridge that deteriorated and was replaced by a fine steel bridge. As ships got larger the need for a bigger Portage Bridge was evident. Today the bridge, which opened for traffice on December 29, 1959, is "the widest and heaviest double deck, vertical lift bridge in the world...."

Quite possibly the Keweenaw Peninsula holds some of the oldest and most intriguing information found in Michigan. The towns that developed came about because of the pure veins of copper discovered in the ground. Copper Harbor, located in the far eastern tip of the peninsula, appeared as a beacon for thousands of incoming miners. Today it beckons the tourist. Fort Wilkins, a preserved U.S. Army Post built to *keep the peace* during the time when miners were flooding the area, stands as a state park since 1923. An interesting sight is the Copper Harbor Lighthouse, built in 1866 as a replacement to the original light built in 1848. Summer and winter are equally fine times to visit Copper Harbor. There are plenty of explorable trails and shorelines and outstanding snowmobile and skiing opportunities. Summer months allow accessibility to Isle Royale National Park, a secluded island north and a little west of Copper Harbor in Lake Superior next to Canadian waters. The National Wilderness Park Service states it is "Michigan's only national wilderness park, ... a preserve set aside in 1931 to protect a prime example of northwoods wilderness. ... The Park was designated an International Biosphere Reserve in 1981 ...." Here is a place to see moose as well as an occasional wolf. Transportation to the island is available by boat or seaplane.

No copper mining occurs on the peninsula today. Communities hold on to the heritage of the area: Lac La Belle, Eagle River, Mohawk, Laurium, Hubbell, Lake Linden and Dollar Bay. The city of Calumet has always been a strong influence on the peninsula. At one time this handsome town saw a population of 70,000 people who came from all parts of the world. When the price for copper plummeted and the Great Depression struck the country, those factors took a big bite out of the economic success of Calumet as well as the entire mining industry in Michigan. In 1989 Calulmet was listed as a National Historic Landmark and was added to the National Register.

The Keweenaw Peninsula is about fifty-miles long and fifteen-miles wide. It is home to people who enjoy the pristine beauty, the best that nature can provide. Michigan's natural wealth still waits for exploration.

Houghton's location is indeed an opportune site. Go north and it is GREAT. Now, go south and it is also GREAT. The Ottawa National Forest is a land of enchantment, in a real sense of the world. It has its own ecosystem, created by Lake Superior's barometric control factor. Spring is often late arriving but when it does arrive, wildflowers scatter splashes of color everywhere they haunt. Summer weather is delightful and calls for the outdoor adventurer to partake of its splendor. The autumn air soon effects the hardwood forests by demanding a change, in color that is. That change is mighty and is celebrated by travelers who always gasp at the varied hues and brilliance of of design. Now winter is the king here, and when the term "Big Snow Country" is exclaimed, it is absolutely correct. Here snow can accumulate up to depths of twenty-five feet, and it is slow in leaving.

The McCormick Wilderness and Sylvania Wilderness are included in Ottawa National Forest, along with so many lakes that a true count is impossible, over three-hundred, many of them are named and many are left untitled. A particular lake to mention is Lake Gogebic, the largest of the lakes in the Upper Peninsula, eighteen-miles long and three-miles wide. It is a fisherman's paradise, where trout, Steelhead, salmon, Large-and-Small-mouth bass and Walleye are waiting for the hook. There is also a group of lakes referred to as the Cisco Chain of Lakes, fifteen lakes with a total of two-hundred-seventy-one miles of shoreline. Swimming and boating are two adventures that can be found in the many lakes, rivers and streams throughout the National Forest. It seems that waterfalls are everywhere.

Elevations vary from six-hundred feet at places along Lake Superior to inland heights reaching over 1,800 feet. With the varied elevation, the chance of good snow sport is excellent, since this area is referred to as the ski capital of the Midwest. There are four superior ski resorts in the area, located near the towns of Ironwood, Bessemer and Wakefield. There are hundreds of miles of snowmobile trails and great space for cross-country skiing. Some trails are groomed while others are available for real country travel.

One great recreation is camping, something that can be done alone or in a group. There are numerous developed campgrounds available all throughout the National Forest. Amenities vary depending on what is available to the camper. That expression "roughing it" can be tamed by using these excellent camping facilities or if that much needed "roughing" experience is the choice, use the trails that reach deep into the forest where primitive sites are available. "With a few minor exceptions the public lands within the Ottawa National Forest are open to back-country camping. Campers should be prepared to pack in a water supply and pack out trash," so the park service comments.

There are communities that provide the cultural needs and supplies for the everyday living demands: Ontonagon, Ironwood, Bessemer, Wakefield and Watersmeet. All of these communities have excellent accommodations for the traveler and vacationer. Each community has very interesting places to go and things to see. Whether skiing is on the agenda or strictly sightseeing, the world's largest artificial ski slide is at Copper Peak near Ironwood, Bessemer and Wakefield, rising two-hundred-forty-one feet above "the crest of Chippewa Hill." The overall length of the slide, as experienced by the skier, is a four-hundred-sixty-nine-foot run. There is the Black River Harbor National Scenic Byway. And some "must see" places are the favorite waterfalls. Rainbow Falls drops forty feet. Conglomerate Falls, which is really an island of rock, is drenched with falling water. Sandstone Falls provides quizzical rock formations and hollows. Potawatomi Falls is one-hundred-thirty feet wide and has a fall space of about thirty feet. Gorge Falls is twenty-nine feet wide and has a twenty-four-foot drop.

East to Watersmeet U.S. Highway 2 leads to Cisco Chain of Lakes and Sylvania Wilderness and Sylvania Recreation Area. The Sylvania confines include thirty-four named lakes, many trimmed with white sandy beaches. Old growth timber is found here, many over "200-years old and some date back to the 1500s."

Pass through the scenic space to Iron River, a small town full of mining lore and vacation attractions, and through the town of Crystal Falls, still in the heart of mining country. Crystal Falls is spread across hilly terrain east and west of the Paint River and provides a tranquil atmosphere plus the spice for a sportsman's adventure. A few miles south is Iron Mountain, home to the "Majestic Pine Mountain Ski Slide." "To date, height of the scaffold is 186 feet, length of the slide is 381 feet, height of the landing hill at Pine Mountain is 349 feet and the length of the landing hill is 426 feet, total length of the entire run is 1,440 feet." There is no belfry here, but if there was, perhaps there might be bats in the belfry, as the Internet Explorer Post 2595 states that "This small town has the second largest bat colony in the world."

The southern most point on the Upper Peninsula is located on Green Bay at Menominee, where a sawmill was first built in 1836 leading to the settlement of a community that incorporated as a city in 1883. The town's name refers to the wild rice that grew at the mouth of the Menominee River, named for the local Native American people, the Menominee, which means wild rice eaters. This city is the county seat of Menominee County, a "leader in the dairy Industry and cheese making," manufacturing with wood, metal and paperboard, and building furniture.

The northern shore of Lake Michigan is the southern edge of Michigan's Upper Peninsula. Escanaba is northeast of Menominee off State Road 35 and east of Kingsford on U.S. Highway 2 and 41 on Little Bay de Noc. The original spelling of Escanaba as E-s-c--o-n-a-w-b-a, as it appeared in Henry Wadsworth Longfellow's *Song of Hiawatha,* which means flat rock. Bay Community College opened its doors in Escanaba in the fall of 1963, filling the need for higher education to the citizens of the area. U.S. Highway 2 goes north along Little Bay de Noc through the communities of Gladstone, Masonville and Rapid River, where the Rapid River and White Fish River empty into Little Bay de Noc. Travel through Ensign, Nahma Junction, Isabella and Garden Corners, maneuvering past Big Bay de Noc and soon the city of Manistique appears. West of town on Road 442 is Indian Lake State Park. The park provides an array of things to experience, since it is located within the confines of Hiawatha National Forest and Lake Superior State Forest. Summer or winter, the park is prepared to be a fun place: fish, hunt, canoe, hike and as weather permits, enjoy cross-country skiing and snowmobiling. There are excellent camping facilities here, too. Indian Lake is the fourth largest lake in the Upper Peninsula. Though it is large in surface area, six-miles long and three-miles wide, it has fairly shallow depths, mostly under fifteen feet. Just east is Manistique, a small town that has been around since 1885, but waited until 1901 to incorporate into a city. You are in serious snowmobile country. As of 1998 Manistique established a city ordinance regulating the vehicular operations of snowmobiles. Snow trails are maintained by a groomer, who keeps them trimmed and detailed for safe riding. Out east on Seul Choix Point, meaning "only choice," is the Seul Choix Point Lighthouse. The story goes that French sailors experiencing severe weather and water conditions on Lake Michigan found shelter in the harbor and named the area *Seul Choix* or "Only Choice." A very fine lighthouse was completed in 1895 and stands today in full operation. The Seul Choix Point Lighthouse Park and Museum provides a hands-on-experience of the maritime history so important to the area.

The Hiawatha National Forest is, in part, north of Manistique, extending toward the eastern edge of the peninsula. The forest includes approximately 880,000 acres and has three of the Great Lakes touching its shores: Lakes Superior, Michigan and Huron. Adventure is at every turn within its boundaries. Pictured Rocks National Lakeshore and Grand Island National Recreation Area are within Hiawatha National Forest. There are six wilderness areas to visit: Big Island Lake, Delirium, Horseshoe Bay, Mackinac, Rock River Canyon and Round Island. Having shoreline created by three Great Lakes, lighthouses are essential and Hiawatha National Forest has ten such lights: Peninsula Point, Point Iroquois, Round Island, Niagara Escarpment, Naomikong Point, Naomikong Suspension Bridge, Grand Island, Spectacle Lake Overlook, Squaw Creek Old Growth Area, and Pendills Creek Fish Hatchery. The forest is a center for hunting, fishing, swimming, hiking, snowmobiling, cross-country skiing and many more activities the adventurer may want to pursue.

Within Hiawatha National Forest is a special place known as Seney National Wildlife Refuge, "established in 1935 for the protection and production of migratory birds and other wildlife." Wetlands make up two-thirds of the refuge. There are "over 200 bird species, 26 fish species and 50 mammals recorded." Start at the Visitor Center and take the leisure seven-mile drive through the marsh and swampland, into the grass and forest area and see such birds as osprey, eagles, loons and trumpeter swans. The Visitor Center is a museum in its own right, providing information and "exhibits on wildlife history, habitat, ecology and management." The Refuge is located north of Manistique, between State Road 94 and 77, off U.S. Highway 2.

Northeast of Manistique is the intersection of U.S. Highway 2 and State Highway 77, gateway to three lakes: North Manistique (small size), Manistique (big size) and South Manistique (medium size). Highway 2 leads to Naubinway, the most northern town on Lake Michigan and back to St. Ignace along a scenic section of highway that parallels Lake Michigan. At St. Ignace the masterful Mackinac Bridge leads back to the Lower Peninsula.

State Parks
And
Recreation Areas

Title	Nearest Municipality
Algonac State Park	Algonac
Aloha State Park	Aloha
Bald Mountain Recreation Area	Lake Orion
Baraga State Park	Baraga
Bay City Recreation Area	Bay City
Bewabic State Park	Crystal Falls
Brighton Recreation Area	Brighton
Brimley State Park	Brimley
Burt Lake State Park	Indian River
Cambridge Historical Park	Cambridge Junction
Cheboygan State Park	Cheboygan
Clear Lake State Park	Atlanta
Craig Lake State Park	Van Riper
Dodge No 4 State Park	Pontiac
Duck Lake State Park	Whitehall
Fayette Historical Park	Garden
Fisherman's Island State Park	Charlevoix
Fort Custer Recreation Area	Battle Creek
Fort Wilkins Historical Park	Copper Harbor
Lake Gogebic State Park	Marenisco
Grand Haven State Park	Grand Haven
Grand Mere State Park	Stevensville
Harrisville State Park	Harrisville
Hartwick Pines State Park	Grayling
W. J. Hayes State Park	Clinton
Higgins Lake, North State Park	Roscommon
Higgins Lake, South State Park	Roscommon
Highland Recreation Area	Highland
Hoeft, P. H. State Park	Rogers City
Hoffmaster, P. J. State Park	Grand Haven
Holland State Park	Holland
Holly Recreation Area	Holly
Indian Lake State Park	Manistique
Indian Lake, West Unit State Park	Manistique
Ionia Recreation Area	Ionia
Interlochen State Park	Interlochen
Island Lake Recreation Area	Brighton

Title	Nearest Municipality
Lake Hudson Recreation Area	Hudson
Lakeport State Park	Port Huron
Laughing Whitefish Falls State Park	Sundell
Leelanau State Park	Northport
Ludington State Park	Ludington
Mackinac Island State Park	Mackinac
Maybury State Park	Northville
F. J. McLain State Park	Calumet
Charles Mears State Park	Pentwater Village
Metamora-Hadley Recreation Area	Metamora
Michilimackinac State Park	Mackinaw City
William Mitchell State Park	Cadillac
Muskallonge Lake State Park	Newberry
Muskegon State Park	Muskegon
Newaygo State Park	Newaygo
Negwegon State Park	Alpena
Old Mill Creek State Park	Mackinaw City
Onaway State Park	Onaway
Orchard Beach State Park	Manistee
Ortonville Recreation Area	Ortonville
Otsego Lake State Park	Gaylord
Palms-Book State Park	Manistique
Pinckney Recreation Area	Pinckney
Petoskey State Park	Petoskey
Pontiac Lake Recreation Area	Pontiac
Porcupine Mountains State Park	Ontonagon
Port Crescent State Park	Port Austin
Proud Lake State Park	Milford
Rifle River Recreation Area	Rose City
Saugatuck State Park	Saugatuck
Seven Lakes State Park	Holly
Silver Lake State Park	Hart
Albert E. Sleeper State Park	Caseville
Sleepy Hollow State Park	Lansing
Sterling State Park	Monroe
Straits-Fr. Marquette National Memorial	St. Ignace
Tahquamenon Falls State Park	Eckerman
Tawas Point State Park	East Tawas
Traverse City State Park	Traverse City
Twin Lakes State Park	Winona
Van Buren State Park	South Haven
Van Riper State Park	Champion
Wagner Falls State Park	Munising
Warren Dunes State Park	Bridgman
Waterloo Recreation Area	Chelsea
J. W. Wells State Park	Cedar River

Title	Nearest Municipality
Wilderness State Park	Mackinaw City
Wilson State Park	Harrison
Yankee Springs Recreation Area	Hastings
Young State Park	Boyne City

Historical Attractions

Title	Location
1839 Historic Courthouse Museum	Berrien Springs
Alfred P. Sloan Museum	Flint
Astor House Museum	Copper Harbor
Benjamin Blacksmith Shop	Mackinac Island
Benzie Area Historical Museum	Benzonia
Bernard Historical Museum	Delton
Biddle House	Mackinac Island
Bradley House Museum and Carriage House	Midland
C. W. Wright Museum of African-American History	Detroit
Cappon House Museum	Holland
Cheboygan County Historical Museum	Cheboygan
Civilian Conservation Corps Museum	Roscommon
Colonial Michilimackinac	Mackinaw City
Cranbrook Education Community	Bloomfield Hills
Dearborn Historical Museum	Dearborn
Delta County Historical Museum	Escanaba
Detroit Historical Museum	Detroit
Edsel and Eleanor Ford House	Grosse Pointe Shores
Ella Sharp Museum	Jackson
Exhibit Museum of Natural History	Ann Arbor
Father Marquette National Memorial	St. Ignance
Fisher Mansion	Detroit
Ford-McNichol Home/Wyandotte Museum	Wyandotte
Fort Brady	Sault Ste. Marie
Fort De Buade Indian Museum	St. Ignace
Fort Mackinac	Mackinac Island
Fort St. Joseph Museum	Niles
Fort Wilkins	Copper Harbor
Gerald R. Ford Museum	Grand Rapids
Frankenmuth Historical Museum	Frankenmuth
Great Lakes Shipwreck Museum	Whitefish Point
Greenmead Historical Park	Livonia
Hanka Homestead Museum	Baraga
Henry Ford Estate—Fair Lane	Dearborn

Title	Location
Henry Ford Museum & Greenfield Village	Dearborn
Herbert H. Dow Historical Museum	Midland
Historic Charlton Park Village and Museum	Hastings
Historical Museum of Bay County	Bay City
Historical Society of Saginaw County	Saginaw
Holland Museum, The	Holland
Honolulu House	Marshall
Huron City Museum	Huron City
Iron County Museum	Caspian
IXL Historical Museum	Hermansville
Jesse Besser Museum	Alpena
Kalamazoo Valley Museum	Kalamazoo
Leelanau Historical Museum	Leland
Little Traverse Historical Museum	Petoskey
Mackinac Bridge Museum	Mackinaw City
Mann House	Concord
Marquette County Historical Museum	Marquette
Marquette Maritime Museum	Marquette
McGulpin House	Mackinac Island
Menominee Range Historical Foundation Museum	Iron Mountain
Michigan Library and Historical Center	Lansing
Michigan Museum of Surveying	Lansing
Michigan State University Museum	East Lansing
Monroe County Historical Museum	Monroe
Museum of Cultural and Natural History	Mount Pleasant
Muskegon County Museum	Muskegon
Navarre-Anderson Trading Post Complex	Monroe
Oakland University's Meadow Brook Hall	Rochester
Old Lighthouse Park and Museum	Presque Isle
Old Mariner's Church	Detroit
Ontonagon County Historical Museum	Ontonagon
Opera House, The	Cheboygan
Plank Alley	Sault Ste. Marie
Plymouth Historical Museum	Plymouth
Port Huron Museum	Port Huron
Presque Isle County Historical Museum	Rogers City
R. E. Olds Transportation Museum	Lansing
River of History Museum	Sault Ste. Marie
Sanilac County Historical Museum and Village	Port Sanilac
SS *Keewatin*	Douglas
Tecumseh Area Historical Museum	Tecumseh
Tibbits Opera House	Coldwater
Tri-Cities Historical Museum	Grand Haven
Van Andel Museum Center of the Public	Grand Rapids
Water Works Building	Manistee

State Symbols

State Flower	Apple Blossom
State Gem	Isle Royal Greenston
State Stone	Petoskey
State Game Mammal	Whitetail Deer
State Bird	Robin
State Fish	Brook Trout
State Reptile	Painted Turtle
State Tree	White Pine
State Soil	Kalakaska

Colleges and Universities

Adrian College, Adrian
Albion College, Albion
Alma College, Alma
Andrews University, Berrien Springs
Aquinas College, Grand Rapids
Baker College, Eight Locations
Calvin College, Grand Rapids
Center for Creative Studies, Detroit
Central Michigan University, Mt. Pleasant
Cleary College, Ypsilanti
Concordia College-Ann Arbor, Ann Arbor
Cornerstone University, Grand Rapids
Davenport College, Grand Rapids
Eastern Michigan University, Ypsilanti
Ferris State University, Big Rapids
Grand Valley State University, Allendale
Hillsdale College, Hillsdale
Hope College, Holland
Kalamazoo College, Kalamazoo
Kendall College/Art & Design, Grand Rapids
Kettering University, Flint
Lake Superior State Univ., Sault Ste. Marie
Lawrence Technological Univ., Southfield

Madonna University, Livonia
Marygrove College, Detroit
Michigan State University, East Lansing
Michigan Technological Univ., Houghton
Northern Michigan University, Marquette
Northwood University, Midland
Oakland University, Rochester
Olivet College, Olivet
Rochester College, Rochester Hills
Saginaw Valley State Univ., University City
Saint Mary's College, Orchard Lake
Siena Heights University, Adrian
Soumi College, Hancock
Spring Arbor College, Spring Arbor
University of Detroit Mercy, Detroit
University of Michigan System*
  *Ann Arbor
  *Dearborn
  *Flint
Walsh College, Troy
Wayne State University, Detroit
Western Michigan University, Kalamazoo
William Tyndale College, Farmington Hills

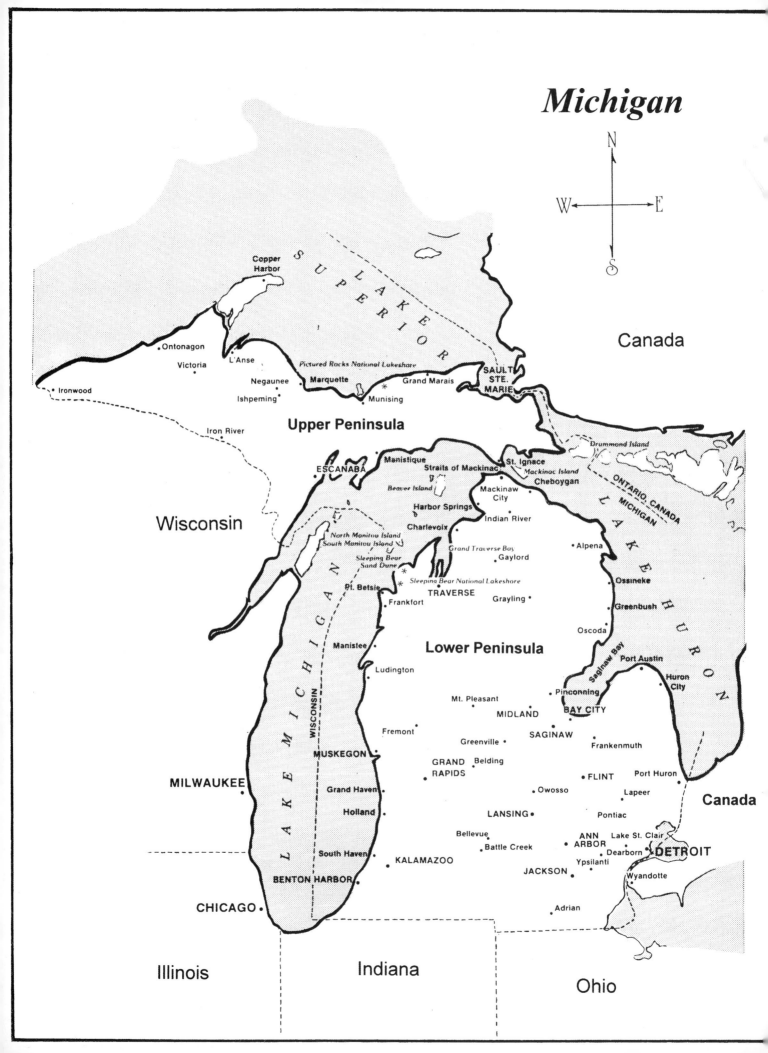